GHOST ATLAS

KURT SLAUSON

GHOST ATLAS

by

Kurt Slauson

All rights reserved. This book or any portion thereof may not be reproduced or used in any manner whatsoever without the express written permission of the publisher except for the use of brief quotations in a book review.

Copyright © Kurt Slauson 2020
Everness Printing 1618

www.kurtslauson.com

ISBN: 978-1-7333526-6-6

Run Amok Books

www.runamokbooks.com

Printed in the USA

for Mom & Dad

Flying Over The Lake In Spring

CONTENTS

v Preface

I. Main Section

Improvised Diagram Tracking the Negative Passage to Shadowy 5
War 6
Prairie Drama Education, Lysistrata 7
First Edition 8
Map 48a 9
Palimpsest #2 [BCE] 10
Ghost Atlas 14

PROSIMETRUM 17

II. Main Section

The Dream Book 39
Fascicles & Versicles 40
TJ Lotto Ticket 43
Caetani, Mezzo Cammin 44
Palimpsest #1 [A – E] 45
The Demon Lap 50
On Paper 51

Appendix 55
Paralipomena, Map 20 59
A Bibliography, Map 48b 61
Gazetteer 63
Coda 64

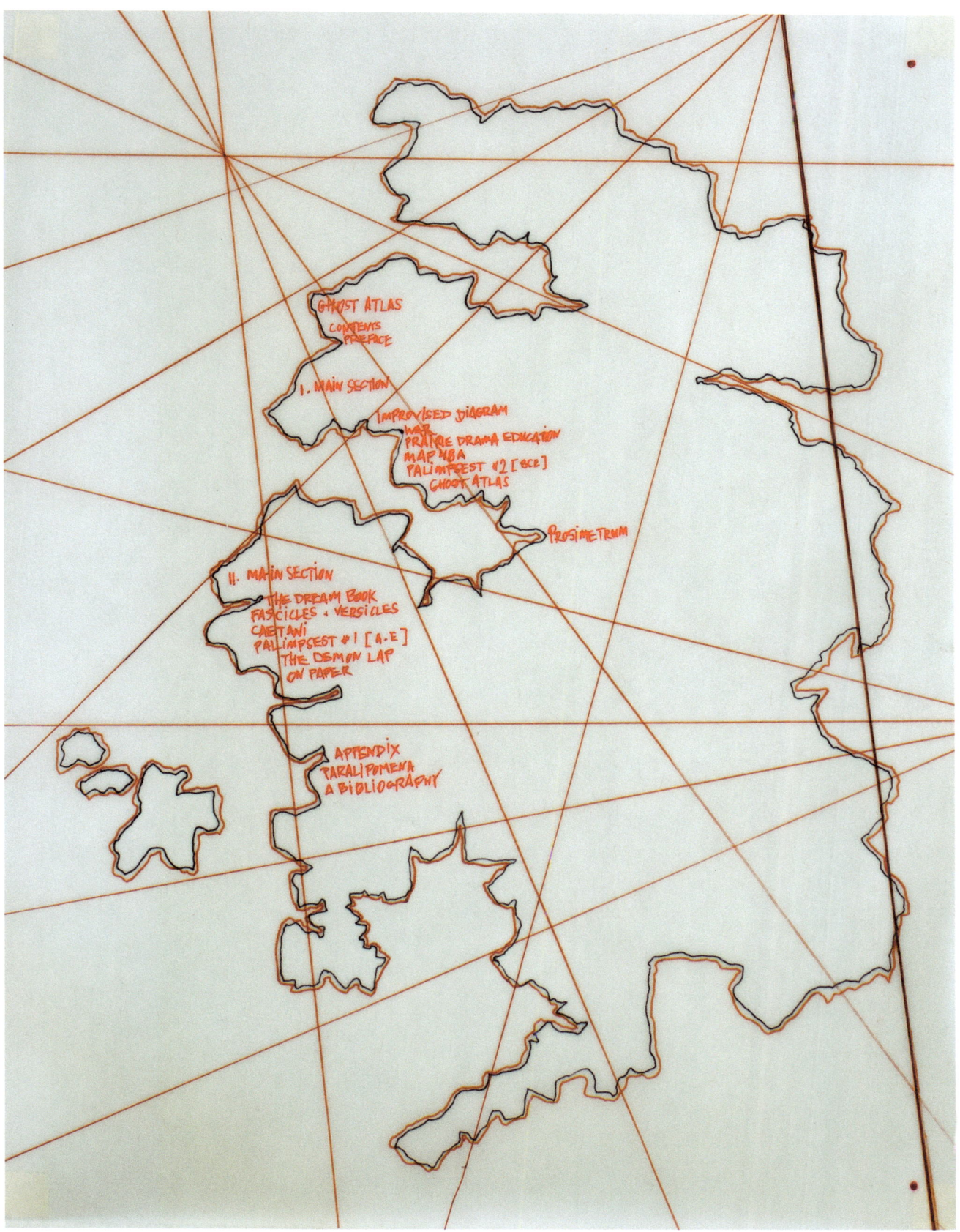

Map #1

Lost At Sea

PREFACE 12.16.18

this book makes a bridge spanning roughly four years' waters and shores up everything surrounding as companion volume to INCUNABULAE and wherever now is.
arcs marks contours revisitations patterns curiosities repeats accidentals, reconstructing of self recovery palimpsestic in nature, amor fati.
interests situated literary history relationality decolonization archive remembrance, having forgotten what I never knew to begin with, encountered in finding, how I have navigated.
how happily-sadly out of place and time I feel, walking anachronism creature.
conversations with history cartography typography poetics general arcana and bibliophilia invocation.
privilege reckoning love song lamentation creative critical homage quarrel thesis jocoseria, writing the perfect day sleeping punctuated by bouts of napping, mancat quilted.
tragi cartoonist autobiog cipher fragments pomo long poem play fanzine—in the timeframe delimited by it and allotted to it, as if found collected, written over top of other work, contained moreless precisely these constituent parts and pieces, some assembly required.
characterized as much by what is not said as by what is of course.

Summer 2016–2020
Kelowna, BC
Syilx Territory

I. MAIN SECTION

It was not long before such hordes of these alien peoples crowded into the island that the natives who had invited them began to live in terror, for the Angles suddenly made an alliance with the Picts whom they had recently repelled, and prepared to turn their arms against their allies.

— Bede, A History of the English Church and People

      sapias, vina liques, et spatio brevi
spem longam reseces. dum loquimir, fugerit invida
aetas. carpe diem, quam minimum credula postero.

— Horace, Odes Book I, XI[1a]

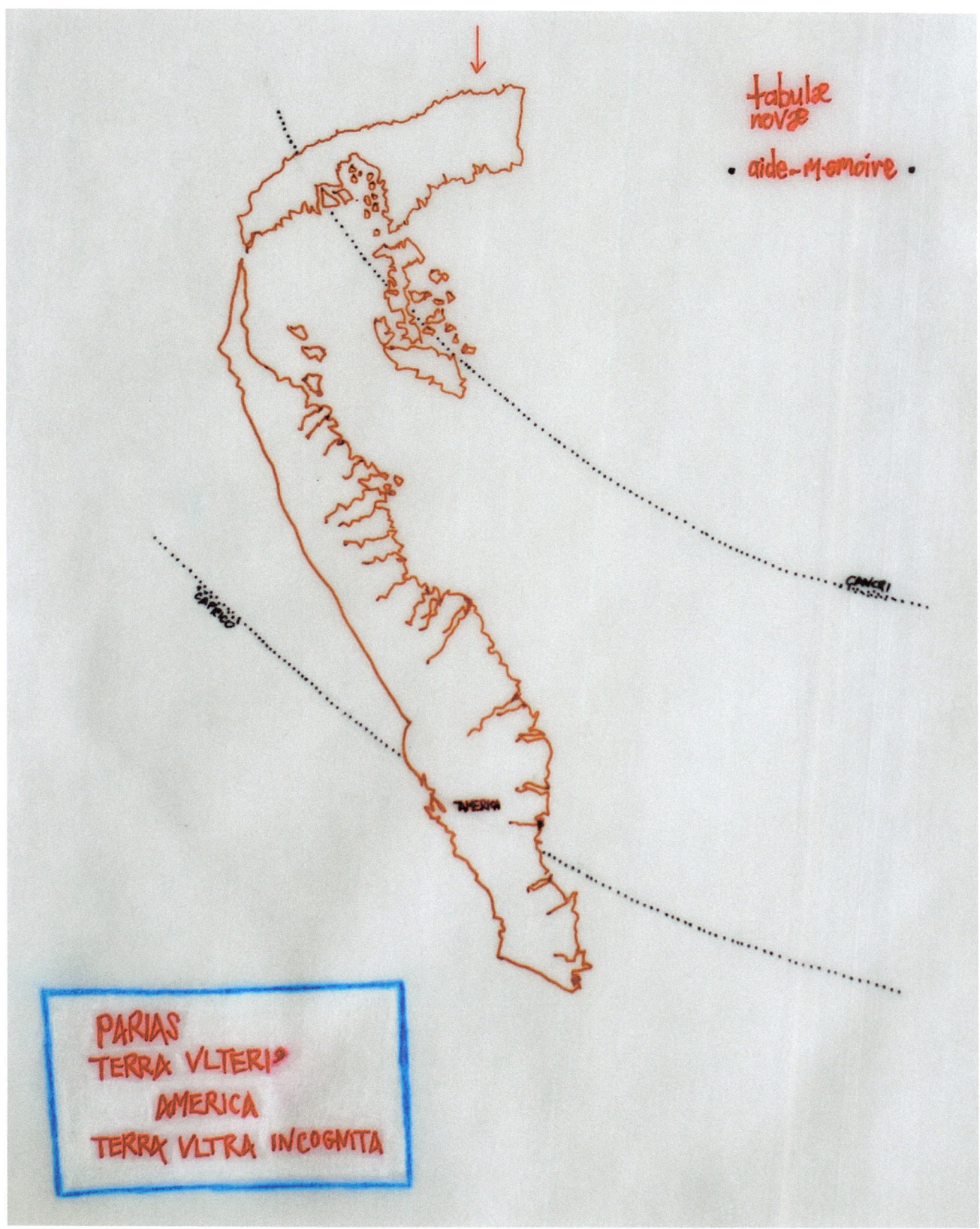

Map #2

IMPROVISED DIAGRAM TRACKING THE NEGATIVE PASSAGE TO SHADOWY

We're going to lee in our handkerchiefs
Tacitly brackets off extra stuff
Dramatize how wide is, villagers

Non-standard measurement, cranky giant
This side is then they made sandals for
The human, human way into it

Goldilocks, little pigs, volcanoes —
Pompeii, Vesuvius, how you doing?
Discipline after school, aftermath.

Architect compelling diaspora
Everything that I have given out
From this place to this place, Canada.

England was where they were coming from
Captaincy tell us who all the land
These oilfields this huge map gold field class

Archetype narrative notion of
Order for family finding who
Journeys there, back in time, strategize.

WAR

one led foe
eye him now
sky bed bow

red old cry
did few out
too how men

low got bad
new she her
two has fed

PRAIRIE DRAMA EDUCATION, Lysistrata

The sky whenat is the combine is at
Yawns like the forgotten onus imbue
Wrote about environments, habitat
Compliance there clients banking renew

More motivated feed me then also
Relationships the learners' key to ask;
This wide talked, engaged lived, elision throw
What faux trial amplified table, toe, task.

Costume wood lighting time theatrical
Book from aren't in a vast dead custody
Hover just like him banished to old dial
In a track violent using one bee

Doing the right thing notion sacrosanct,
Judge play in while I wasted questions thanked.

FIRST EDITION
SHEET 72 ¹/₇ EAST HALF

SURVEYS AND MAPPING BRANCH

REFERENCE
_____

Chumasha	I
Siouan	
Iroquoian	
Papuan	
Mande	
Mixe–Zoque	
Indo–Aryan	7
Oto–Manguean	
Koreanic	
Arawakan	
Tupian	
West Germanic	
Northwest Caucasian / NE	13
Trans–New Guinean	
Algic	
Yeniseian	
Chukotko–Kamchatkan	
Na–Dene	
Baltic	19
Iranian	
Uto–Aztecan	
Japonic	
Mayan	
Khosian	
Tungusic	25
Hmong–Mien	
Sign	
Eskimo Aleut	
Celtic	
Kartvelian	
Creole	31
Pidgin	
Mongolic	
Nilo–Saharan	
Semitic	
Tai–Kadai	
Slavic	37
Turkic	
Romance	
Niger–Congo	
Austronesian	
Sino–Tibetan	
Austroasiatic	43
Altaic	
Uralic	
Indo–European	

MAP 48a

       Bound is the boatless man — Viking proverb

hen swept the sands
      those beaches
        This West
combing over

hereinafter
mine
decline and fall
    in these
plays and masques
     O, Jonson!

Tied the skiff to the
     house
and planted, tried
     to plant

here where the
     apple ducks
      Malus Mallard
into seed sleep

shored and coughs along
vellum career of
     Autumn's breach

The old ones
     still legible
dance the damned
     dance
they do
     dance
the damned dance

+ students

PALIMPSEST #2

[2B]

&

i   ii i i i i i
Ishango bone, Congo
    i   i   i
Baboon fibula
i i i i i   i i i
irresistible

&

tree =
"bird holder"

&

Anthropic principle

alcohol
[become]
atheist guide to
self–flagellation

both
much that was
sacrificed
and
much that was taken
away
from me

&

sanctimonious

— fine line —

flippant

[2C]

&

automythogenic

surface : amuse
depth : amaze

universal hegemony
of assent

———

some sort of
what to call it

adapt and explain
fit and fluency

&

dark optimism
bright pessimism

Flashes of light
[and]
glimmers

———

books a
promise of
promise

where found
falutin
love song of the
sounded

polished poop
and gilded lily
whole necklace of potatoes
alway

[poetry place for all poetry]

[2E]

&

willful intensity
combined
patient resolve

walking the clouds
Yggdrasil suffers agony
more than men know

"a language is
a dialect with
an army and a navy"

having nothing to say
they said it interminably

astonishingly grand with an
air of engaging scruffiness
makes it all the more charming

Celtic toilette, thoor Ballyphallus
Neverness, well, it's got all these
different faces but it's the same

goddamned war Carloman

Charles Martel
Charles Magus
Charlemagne
Magna Carta
Charles Mingus

inexorable
Adamo me fecit
Fatta a mano
Faute de mieux

as it was narrated to me
by an especially peculiar Man
glossd "EK"

"history is the
inevitable casualty
of empire"

jongleur, critical juncture
hypotheses arrange,

and in the long patina grew
traject of change that we drew

GHOST ATLAS

> Who falls from all he knows of bliss,
> Cares little into what abyss. — Lord Byron

I
And then trapped in a lone cold note boat
Borne contumely wayfaring the ribald wind

These four trees have seen me scarring myself
Grim amalgam of daydreamings

Lost handsomely harmfully won fire back at cost
Retire to the glazy dim green reach of me

II
Now to chart the lostness loom
Now to brighten the fecund field behold

When great sadnesses at work refund
The sunny sailorman's summer solstice

High riding washed awashed aghast at best
Into garden light gloaming glossed beckons

III
Playing good children the drum of the draft
Mapped as though countries were watching

Belonging to that best land best voic'd O tack
These fevered beings aloft and unfettered arise

Whole the place over cover dawn to bright might
That we go there better in peace and in kindness

IV
Divest unto silence capricious fair daisy
Cavorting the foam of a blind teaspoon sea

Where go'st ask nothing ludibrium pelagis
Some unfound forgiveness collated disappeared

Forever as never is charted cold eye being
Deep inland cries undone freedom ring

Carta Marina

PROSIMETRUM

I have four degrees of force and four of weight as well as four degrees of movement and four of time. I want to use these degrees and augment or reduce them according to necessity in my imagination, in order to discover the will of the laws of nature.

— Leonardo da Vinci

Madrid MS. I, f. 152 r.
See also Madrid MSS I–II, IV, p.145
THE MADRID CODICES
ed. Ladislao Reti
5 vols. New York, 1974

Map #3[2]

would that I could again lay
down beside you there weep
with such sorrow and weep
with such joy for to hold to each
where we weep

we
would that
we

we
don't

everyone
is bad

we
do

just our one
puny voice

[warbling]
inexhaustible

But I had to
leave

all that
behind

rascal hiccough

dicks

Raskolnikov

survey

Vaclav Havel
    tbr "Summertime Meditations"

———

Kakisubata : Noh
(The Iris)
episode 9 Tales of
Joyce's Finnegan's

———

Derrida heliotrope
        Boccaccio Calandrino

    wht myth

———

dingbat
…

apogee
peonage
fideistic
…

"belief templates"
      DFW
…

Eyak language extinction
…

kenning
heiti

———

Poem

        Pete Balakian
"Hart Crane in LA 1927"

6 trips by ferry HC³

That now six times these straights have
        cross'd
and do long for your leap, and but for what
        we've lost
I urge that toward this motion wild spent
        and terrific
I'd find quiet in the cold green brine North
        Pacific

…

frolicked in the afterglow
in a land called
meant to be

Neruda   Canto General
"Transgeographic suprahistorical"

1666 – Annus Mirabilis
———

pelf

…

MUSEUM OF ME (toward)

I have mourned you loving
in each and every iota
of your cunning

Every record, every book
every placement

much ado
in these trees

shall be my books
and in their barks
I'll character

extravagant
encomium

———

Endings
Beginnings
Transitions

―――

Limner

rumbustious

―――

Divine Comedy Fridge Magnet

1 he exalts in himself
2 he exalts in others
3 all other parties

———

*** LAND OF PUNT
    "Eternal dumpster fire"

XLV
not here and Imladris

Doughnut lumpf
His was the great
cadavared agar flop
in the great assholery
& etc. venom tongued
cheatorangydusted
bloated groaning
sewer, mucous I cough
scum of mind
scum of earth

where I stopped, lost
Usurper Shithole Assault

———

energetic exegesis
[hexa

peculation
perquisites

bolo tie
logotype

Monotype Ehrhardt
linotype pilgrim

Senex (Sea?)
Legacy (leg)]

Suda
Compass

―――

This significant intaglio
breach bends
Contesting the book as
sacrosanct, sanctimonious

Fetishized object
Marginalia rubric
poets eyes profits

…

Shakespeare's Bacon Chipper

Wait What
What's non-fiction
Fiction's not real
I never get that right
Fiction's not real

(late Whitman)

―――

redolent
recusant
redactive

―――

I didn't burn bridges
I just took off every other plank
for this here fire, see!

———

grandiloquacious
not knot naught
choropleth mapping

eat quirk
aporetic duplication
curt castellan
                                          1396
Hal O' the Wynd
"a most unusual share of strength"

excursus
ludic

———

Shelley
       Who with the devil doth
       rage & revel   [frag]

       Laon&Cythna

How calamity
Befel family

Great Tew
Oxford

James > Iacomus > Iacobus

6 DeiGratiaScotorum

———

Culann's Hound
my riastrad
piss
wash
regret

———

Loki stealing
time

silly
really

calumnious
periplus

domains where
faking it

is real
the real

———

GM Hopkins
      "chance left free to act"

Milton
Eikon
Sidney "Arcadia"

cynghanedd, Hiraeth

———

big trucks
sucks

gashog trucks
sad man pucks

parking lots
stucks

noise your shots
bucks

———

The History of History
A History of Histories
History of Historians

colonial lag myth

unsettling150.ca

1969 White Paper, Red

DOL/INM > 10 princips[4]

"Rights as defined
by the Federal Policy"

Propaedeutic to a
countervailing distortion

Werner Herzog
    "to extend sympathy where it has
not been"

Beatus ille
"Happy the man"
Horace, II Epode

Ghost Atlas

falsehoods
dissemblings
prevarications
lies

repristination

Icosahedron
Platonic solids
Archimedean solids

agitata

Turning over rocks

NEW REVIEW

…

Long Poems

insufferable
authentic

The Complete Atlas of
Proserpine Salad

Francesco Colonna, 1499
· Hypnerotomachia Poliphili ·

Lo Compasso da Navigare
1296

JDerrida · Meister Eckhart

GENERAL ESTORIA
Alfonso X El Sabio, Castile
1252-84

[troianalexandrina]

Verica of Atrebates
                    vertical
                    of vertebrates
                    ventricle

...

    RDuncan/EPound

"out of key with his time"
Gemisthus Plethon
trobar clus
12th c
Albigensian gnosis
Kabbalah
neo-Platonism
Plotinus
Porphyry
Proclus
Iamblichus
> Eleusis
Gassin
Spirit Euterpe
Rosicrucian John Heydon
      > Bulverton Hill

...

endonym
exonym

"adjectival floridity"

supervenience
haecceity

Prometheus

…

because cartography is one of those supreme horizons where science and art intersect

where passes the [novelistic] convention in which the writing becomes a metaphor of its own textuality, of textuality itself

…

Coleridge BL
167
Huge fragments vaulted

Zuk A9
     Cavalcanti
     Donna mi priegha
     Canzone
     Kapital 1–13
     Value Price Profit

Allen: electrons & waves

Duncan
Whitehead

…

correct
factual
accurate
verifiable

…

cold note boat

———

as full of suggestion
as inconclusive

O how I have missed you

[letter]

Serious Joy
He was talking to his book when

Forgetting
where they went

Remember
Remember in the book of
Remember the time
Remember what happened

Ephemera
"memory in motion"

Library as Wish-List

It's all I'd really
like to know
honestly, fall.

haven't I said
I've done that
enough enough?

unbridled calamity
undone corded bales
w no Dover Beach
to long, to mourn
too long Re: member
ship
cancellation
to unsubscribe

this here
to hear
to listen
I, Crispinly
cites sites sights

It was difficult
to live
but to make

during which time
mind and body
was not kind

would be remiss
to let that
persist

Dispatches/Orisons

II. MAIN SECTION

Fragments are not included unless they add something of typographical value to the entries under a particular printer; and they are not included in the index by authors, for their presence there would be merely misleading to one looking for the text of a work.

— Herman Ralph Mead, INCUNABULA IN THE HUNTINGTON LIBRARY
    San Marino, California 1937[5]

Break, break, break,
  At the foot of thy crags, O sea!
But the tender grace of a day that is dead
  Will never come back to me.

— Alfred, Lord Tennyson

Map #4

THE DREAM BOOK

The part
is me

I look the part
is me

are going over
being through

passage

whereon
is written

over and
above

writes itself —

rare to one
finding

how I did
toward
further

live onto
here

how
still standing

to stand
it go

that cannot
repair

and so
forcibly

moved to turn
turn

FASCICLES & VERSICLES

§

Wrecking Ball Tumbleweed

when the only surety is
anyone but me
Then why not me

» connect (end)

[dactylic pentameter]

§

The Blind Factory

hugs
bee
bugs

How when you get in close
all you see is
toil and turmoil

§

Hunnic Ring

science of stupid
Poetry (myth) making
bombs of Science
When I Heard Learn'd Astro contra Science
war metonymy
Ethics of Science

§

Will To Flower: Four Instants

wilt to power   [incidence incidents]

1625
Nicholas Ferrar est. Anglican
community at Little Gidding
— broken up by Puritans 1647

Wentworth's policy of "Thorough"
    in Ireland

Antonio Malatesti   1638
        La Tina, Milton

Pasquino
"what the barbarians left
undone the Barberini did"

§

Feedback Loop
Pound reading Pound
reading Susan Howe, m'elevasti
        Pound cadence
Howe reading Howe

———

texts   Cantos 81, II, XC-II
               Singularities "3 Taking the Forest"

Emily Dickinson's three dog night[6]
What is Reading? What is Translation?

Sounding poetry

§

Notes Toward An Ordinary Fiction

"if fate is nigh, don't let me die, in this strange country"

Pedagogy Saints they

Narcissus me

heart of darkness Childe

      IV
For, what with my whole world-wide wandering,
  What with my search drawn out thro' years, my hope
  Dwindled into a ghost not fit to cope
With that obstreperous joy success would bring,
I hardly tried now to rebuke the spring
  My heart made, finding failure in its scope.

These are the chartings
                        [omit]
These are the flota
The timbers

slaver enslavd
shame coffee shame cod
shame tea shame tobacco
shame sugar shame oil
pure products crazy whale of shame

Never we'll
how go

Far have sights
own know

TJ LOTTO TICKET • Monticello • July 4, 1819

01
all men
all men
all men
      are created equal

not men
not men pendo

      are created equal

not there slave
some men

all men
all men
      are created equal

women
{wo[m(e)n]} pendere
all women

and men
emend lawmen amen slave
declare

not men
they
      are created equal

other, wise women
declare

CAETANI, Mezzo Cammin

This Boniface
Benedetto Caetani Dante

this Firenze Sermoneta Ninfa
    Roma Anagni

"took no care for the highest office or
the holy orders that were his"

Leone
this pi this zero
this Wall St.
this exile
this freedom
Vernon BC Canada[7]
this prison
Europe
this Rome

how unpopulist
this Islam you write
Language and debt
"world famous exiles"

how unlikely
did you dream this
deeply unlikely
resiliency this
– di tante foglie –
Teacher Sveva?

as did Boniface VIII
known by its incipit
[Nightmare] Avignon   1309
COMINCIA LA COMEDIA DI
dante alleghieri di fiorenze
• editio princeps 1472 •
Johann Numeister & Evangelista Angelini da Trevi
Foligno
slander

This hedged-in Paradise
This hell
    Paradiso 33.142
    Gower, Confessio II 2861-
        3027-8

tour museum artefacts
art of the haunted house
thesaurus absconditus
what left behind
what found what lost
what loss,
library students #order

The sun on my face
all that lives
in terror

PALIMPSEST #1

[1A]

¶ everything is here
in a way
all artfully placed
by no one design

¶

In each word
is a song that
time forgot

¶

There is a forever kind of talk
That sees the codes
[fraud/woe]
Beset with

And disinclined

¶

Time is
running out
is always
is least
understood –
Sort of
like nothing
that didn't
happen

[1B]

¶ dragging these
weights around
to never
recover
things –
from them
how never
to have wanted
this these ways

¶

elocutions
of the
wandless
wizmatist   the
———   absolute
                         stupendour
genuine   !
authentic
truth

¶

working toward
some semblance
of order

to reside
in stupefaction
and awe

reminiscence

I am painfully
aware
I'm not
welcome
over there

[1C]

¶ a process
about
a process
about
a process

¶

This time
last year
I wasn't
sitting here
doing
the same
thing

¶

never   and
where   there
I'll   and
ever   everywhere
Belong   where
———
unless
that be
here

¶

Is this pain
is this not pain
I don't know
I don't
want to make
too much
of pain

[1D]

¶ I
looked
for you
every
where
but you are
not
here

¶

I
would be
deliriously
happy
to do
that
with you

¶

floating on
zeros
across the
board
like bubbles
in a
fish bowl

¶

being grateful
―――――
being
diminished

[1E]

¶ good hard life
hard good life

hard goods
hard woods

[centre] The Fool
Leo [drawn]

¶

Estrangement
folks
is
nothing new
unless it's
new
to you

¶

To live one's lie
uncomfortably
spectacularly,
now that is
something.

Lived poetically
But without the
poems.

Unlikeable people
making beautiful
things

am sorry

I started with
      a pot
And picked a plant

      thought

   for that pot

——   Rhymer

slant
thought

THE DEMON LAP

> And be among her cloudy trophies hung. — John Keats

1
I did the demon lap

And landed

where no me

e'er stood
where

you were not at the end
dear thine
tho I thanked you,
was fraught.

I looped the lap hooped
Lapped it up flew

You feared and
withdrew knowing

where I was going
where failed
failed at feeling

stopped
and then shutting
is closing and

cutting your book
furthest through me.

2
all
going all round

then I counted and

Saw in the darkness mount
      the light and green
         in the light in the dark waves

Over light
there
our beautiful bright

I find lamentable sad became thy
      warm sight

I spring love to greet
you once
      aeternam omnibus

Here down miracle garden

ON PAPER

Shopping for loans here
rags pick'd these

uncatalogued
each to locating

this one writes my smoke
and this one sums my drink

this one writes regret
and these triumphal innocence

where this writes
loss the o'erpowering

dank where lies
its sacral visage shot up

this when my father
in lucid connection

to narrative said
it is a triumph

of me, inside
when my father turns in

and this shop tattooed
on bones with eyes

the linen skeins
the dragon red

the names change
as ragpicker plies

viral piratical
non-territorial vouch

that life lives
on life

To be continued
is all I ever really

wanted to do
and see

set free in you among
peoples moved

along lines altogether
scraped writes a

pulpy vat adrift
hewn from the mists

emissary as it
crumbles all around us

and stands there
from an antique land

portolan promotion of
accuracy

perpetuation of
inaccuracy

All the work
I haven't done

it reminds me
of me

whereof these places
where measur'd

along regret
to have missed

and treasur'd
where I have loved

this vast old tree
underneath

Visitant

APPENDIX

Paralipomena, Map 20 59
A Bibliography, Map 48b 61
Gazetteer 63
Coda 64

Measurement began our might.

— W.B. Yeats

Ic on wincle gefrægn   weaxan nathwæt,
þindan ond þunian,   þecene hebban;
on þæt banlease   bryd grapode,
hygewlonc hondum,   hrægle þeahte
5   þrindende þing   þeodnes dohtor.

— Riddle 45 (or 43)[1b]

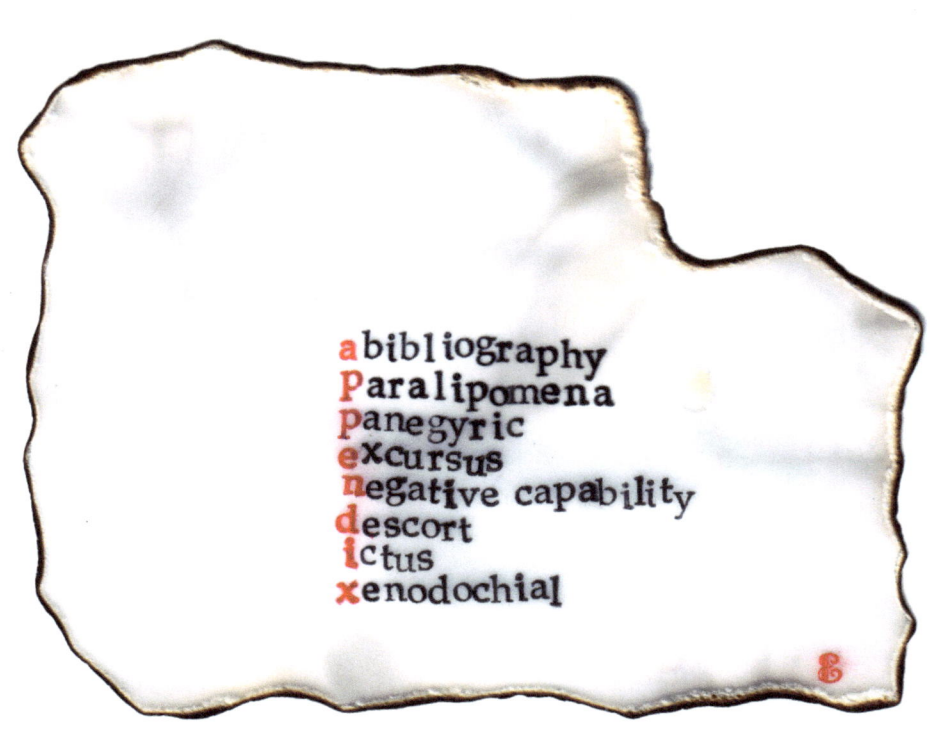

1618 Map #5 attr. Ó Sléibhín · Fear Manach Personal Papers [XIX]

Ink on vellum paper   11 x 15 cm (4½ x 6 in)

The only extant copy of *1618 Map #5*. Letters not used qwjzkf. Fragment indicates gratitude projection frequencies of unknown extent or limit. Patience, humility, compassion, understanding—resolutions deferred here murmured "third bird heard alight aloft a word," scent rent went bent, meant happy through neverness though calling it new, chancing the dim light morning blue, outwardly shew great orison and fiddled fire, the hue in a fatuous wind, sound of a quire.

Map #5

PARALIPOMENA Map 20

☞

[1] Translations—differents—because they are so.

[a] Horace:

Show wisdom. Strain clear the wine; and since life is brief, cut short far-reaching hopes! Even while we speak, envious Time has sped. Reap the harvest of to-day, putting as little trust as may be in the morrow!
—trans. C.E. Bennett [cf. Horace]

or,

  Be wise, strain clear the wine
  And prune the rambling vine
Of expectation. Life's short. Even while
  We talk Time, grudging, runs a mile.
    Don't trust tomorrow's bough
    For fruit. Pluck this, here, now.
—trans. James Michie [cf. Horace]

[b] Riddle 45 (ASPR), question or 43 (or 44) because there is unknown how many precisely and/or were intended:

I saw in a corner   something swelling,
Rearing, rising   and raising its cover.
A lovely lady,   a lord's daughter,
Buried her hands   in that boneless body,
Then covered with a cloth   the puffed-up creature.
—trans. Richard Wilbur [cf. Delanty]

or,

I have heard of something that grows in a corner,
swelling and standing up, lifting up its covering.
Upon that boneless thing a proud-minded woman
gripped with her hands; with her garment a lord's daughter
covered the swollen thing.
— [cf. Treharne (76)]

☞

[2] Loving shoutout to Michael Roderick • creator, Mood Area 52 @ www.rocketboyarts.com • for first inscribing the red baboon's ass, ca. 1991.

☞

[3] Grateful to Ed Skoog • author of TRAVELERS LEAVING FOR THE CITY (2020) @ coppercanyonpress.org • for publishing my poem "Six Trips By Ferry To Vancouver Island Hart Crane, To You" in MONSTER: THE MONTHLY BROADSHEET OF NEW POEMS, issue 3, New Orleans, LA, 2000. Written '95-6 in transition from Montana to BC, in a deep spell of Shelleyan Craneishness, itself insufferably long, was part of a larger ungainly suite called "The Laughter Invention" the manuscript drafts of which remain ensconced in the archive • a memento mori •

❡

⁴ Defenders of the Land & Idle No More movements; for more information and advocacy for the rights of Indigenous Peoples in North America, check out • www.ienearth.org • lim'limpt

❡

⁵ Herman Ralph Mead, purchased at used bookstore High Browse Books (great name, sadly now out of business); owner knocked me ten dollars off his asking price for this volume; "Thanks!" I said, "because it takes a special kind of nerd!"

❡

⁶ Emily Dickinson's three dog night: —from my time in graduate schools, the trace of research that didn't ("all in the diffidence that faltered") happen, a palimpsest, writing over memory. Poet Susan Howe's work with Emily Dickinson's manuscripts; met her at lecture/reading Dr. Chris Beach held at UMT, she was brilliant and lovely; lectured abt EDs mss (what came out of MY ED and would become BIRTHMARK) and read from SINGULARITIES, unforgettable; after party Dr. Wm. Bill Bevis' home, chatted with her that she is "dyed in the wool" a New Englander, her communion with ED, signed my copy of EUROPE OF TRUSTS, Missoula 1994; and also — «…after reading a magazine article about Indigenous Australians in which it was explained that on cold nights they would customarily sleep in a hole in the ground while embracing a dingo (wild dog). On colder nights they would sleep with two dogs and, if the night was freezing, it was a 'three dog night'…»

❡

⁷ Caetani Cultural Centre, Vernon BC
I had the privilege and pleasure of working here for a month, an art history treasure—the Caetani family story, dating back to 10thc. Rome. Following on 25 years of confinement at home by her mentally unstable mother, Sveva Caetani emerged into the world in her mid-forties mostly bereft, and went on to become an extraordinary teacher and artist; is a hero of resiliency & testimony to the healing power of art. "Mezzo Cammin," literally "half journey," written 1842 by Henry Wadsworth Longfellow, American poet and translator of Dante. In her painting-poem series, RECAPITULATION (1989), Sveva Caetani invokes Dante's DIVINE COMEDY in a spiritual and aesthetic collaboration with the legendary poet who was exiled by, and subsequently did much to malign, her many-times great grandfather, Pope Boniface VIII. Grateful to our local literary arts collective • www.inspiredwordcafe.com • for the opportunity to read this poem in person to the living poet, Daphne Marlatt, who very much inspired it; thereat warmly signed my copy of READING SVEVA, her breathtaking poetic journey through Sveva's life and art.

https://www.caetani.org
https://en.wikipedia.org/wiki/Sveva_Caetani/
https://en.wikipedia.org/wiki/Leone_Caetani/
https://en.wikipedia.org/wiki/Caetani

❡

A BIBLIOGRAPHY Map 48b

MAPS

Atkinson, Sam, ed. Great City Maps. New York: DK Publishing, 2016.
Brotton, Jerry. A History of the World in 12 Maps. New York: Viking Penguin, 2012.
Clark, John O.E. Maps that Changed the World. London: Batsford, 2015.
Clarke, Victoria, ed. Map: Exploring the World. London: Phaidon Press Ltd., 2015.
Collins Bartholomew Ltd. Collins World Atlas: Illustrated Edition. Glasgow: HarperCollins, 2013.
Esri Map Book volume 31. Redlands, CA: Esri Press, 2016.
Hardwick, F.C. & Cyril Midgley. Understanding Maps. Toronto/Vancouver: Clarke, Irwin & Co. Ltd., 1961.
Hofmann, Catherine, Hélène Richard & Emmanuelle Vagnon. The Golden Age of Maritime Maps: When Europe Discovered the World. Richmond Hill, ON: Firefly, 2012.
Imhof, Eduard. Schweizerischer Mittelschulatlas. Orell Füssli Graphische Betriebe AG, Zürich, 1976.
Mattéoli, Francisca. Map Stories: The Art of Discovery. London: ILEX, 2016.
Onion, The. Our Dumb World: Atlas of the Planet Earth – 73rd edition. Scott Dikkers, ed. New York: Little-Brown & Co., 2007.
Portinaro, Pierluigi & Franco Knirsch. The Cartography of North America: Mapping the New World 1500-1800. East Bridgewater, MA: JG Press/World Publications Group, 2015.
Royal Canadian Geographical Society. The Canadian Geographic Atlas of Canada. Toronto: HarperCollins, 2014.
SendPoints Publishing Co., Ltd. The Art of Cartographics: Designing the Modern Map. London: Goodman, 2017.
The Reader's Digest Complete Atlas of the British Isles. London: Reader's Digest Assoc. Ltd., 1965.

LEGEND

Alighieri, Dante. The Divine Comedy of Dante Alighieri: A Verse Translation by Allen Mandelbaum. Notes by Allen Mandelbaum & Gabriel Marruzzo with Larry Magnus. Illus. Barry Moser. New York: A Bantam Classic ed., Bantam Books, 1982.
———. The Divine Comedy. Trans. ed. intr. Robin Kirkpatrick. New York: Penguin Group, 2013.
Ariosto, Ludovico. Orlando Furioso. Trans. Barbara Reynolds. Harmondsworth, Middlesex: Penguin Books, 1975.
Barnard, Mary. Sappho: A New Translation. Fw. Dudley Fitts. Berkeley/LA: U of California P, 1958.
Beach, Christopher. The ABC of Influence: Ezra Pound and the Remaking of American Poetic Tradition. Berkeley: U of California P, 1992.
Bevis, William W. Mind of Winter: Wallace Stevens, Meditation, and Literature. Pittsburgh, PA: U of Pittsburgh P, 1988.
Bowers, Fredson. Principles of Bibliographic Description. Princeton, NJ: Princeton UP, 1949.
Bringhurst, Robert. The Elements of Typographic Style v4.0 Vancouver: Hartley & Marks, 2012.
Caetani, Sveva. Recapitulation: A Journey. Heidi Thompson, Angela Gibbs Peart & Dennis Butler, Eds. Vernon, BC: Coldstream Books, 1995.
Carson, Luke. "'The Malady of Ideality': Mallarmé's Igitur in John Ashbery's 'Fragment'." Texas Studies in Literature and Language, v59 n1 Spring 2017. Austin: U of Texas P, 2017.
Cave, Roderick & Sara Ayad. The History of the Book in 100 Books: The Complete Story from Egypt to E-book. Fw. Sidney E. Berger & Michelle V. Cloonan. Richmond Hill, ON: Firefly, 2014.
Connell, Charles. World Famous Exiles. Feltham, Middlesex: Odhams Books, 1968.
Crystal, David. The Stories of English. London: Penguin-Allen Lane, 2004.
Cunningham, Valentine. The Victorians: An Anthology of Poetry & Poetics. Oxford: Blackwell Publishers Ltd., 2000.
Dawson, Paul. Creative Writing and the New Humanities. New York & London: Routledge/Taylor-Francis, 2005.
Delanty, Greg and Michael Matto, eds. The Word Exchange: Anglo-Saxon Poems in Translation. New York: W.W. Norton & Company, 2011.
Denny, Norman & Josephine Filmer-Sankey. The Bayeux Tapestry: The Norman Conquest 1066. London: Collins, 1966.
Dewey, John. Democracy and Education: An Introduction to the Philosophy of Education (1916). Ithaca, NY: Cornell University Library, 2009.

Emmerson, Richard K. and Sandra Clayton-Emmerson, eds. Who's Who in the Middle Ages, 2 vols. New York & London: Routledge/Taylor-Francis, 2006.

Falk, John H. & Lynn D. Dierking. The Museum Experience Revisited. Walnut Creek, CA: Left Coast Press, 2014.

Falk, John H. Identity and the Museum Visitor Experience. Walnut Creek, CA: Left Coast Press, 2009.

Fox, Margalit. The Riddle of the Labyrinth: the Quest to Crack an Ancient Code. New York: Ecco, 2013.

Goldsmith, Kenneth. Uncreative Writing: Managing Language in the Digital Age. New York: Columbia UP, 2011.

Horace [Quintus Horatius Flaccas]. The Odes and Epodes. Trans. C.E. Bennett. Cambridge, MA & London: The Loeb Classical Library, Harvard UP, William Heinemann Ltd., 1960.

———. The Odes of Horace. Trans. James Michie, Intr. Rex Warner. New York: The Orion Press, 1963.

Houston, Keith. The Book: A Cover-to-Cover Exploration of the Most Powerful Object of Our Time. New York: W.W. Norton & Co., 2016.

———. Shady Characters: Ampersands, Interrobangs and Other Typographical Curiosities. London: Particular Books-Penguin, 2013.

Howe, Susan. My Emily Dickinson. Berkeley: North Atlantic Books, 1985.

———. Singularities. Hanover, NH & London: Wesleyan/UP of New England, 1990.

———. The Birth-mark: Unsettling the Wilderness in American Literary History. Hanover, NH & London: Wesleyan/UP of New England, 1993.

———. The Nonconformist's Memorial. New York: New Directions, 1989.

Marlatt, Daphne. Reading Sveva. Vancouver: Talon Books, 2016.

Mathur, Ashok, Jonathan Dewar & Mike DeGagné. Cultivating Canada: Reconciliation Through the Lens of Cultural Identity. Ottawa: Aboriginal Healing Foundation, 2011.

Mathur, Ashok. The First White Black Man. Vancouver: MonoGraph, 2016.

McCaffery, Steve. Slightly Left of Thinking: Poems Texts and Post-Cognitions. Tucson: Chax Press, 2008.

Mead, Herman Ralph. Incunabula in the Huntington Library. Los Angeles: Adcraft Press, 1937.

Miller, Christanne, ed. Emily Dickinson's Poems: As She Preserved Them. Cambridge, MA & London: Belknap/Harvard UP, 2016.

Munday, Jeremy. Introducing Translation Studies : Theories and Applications. London/New York: Routledge, 2001.

Okigbo, Christopher. Labyrinths: Poems; with Path of Thunder. London, Ibadan, Nairobi: Heinemann/Mbari, African Writers Series 62, 1971.

Palmer, Michael. "I Do Not." The Promises of Glass. New York: New Directions, 2000.

Parks, Tim. Medici Money: Banking, Metaphysics, and Art in Fifteenth-century Florence. New York & London: W.W. Norton & Co., 2005.

Pyle, Forest. Art's Undoing: In the Wake of a Radical Aestheticism. New York: Fordham UP, 2013.

Rainey, Lawrence, S. Ezra Pound and the Monument of Culture: Text, History, and the Malatesta Cantos. Chicago & London: U of Chicago P, 1991.

Raymond, Marcel. From Baudelaire to Surrealism: Translated from the French (1933). London: Peter Owen Ltd., 1957.

Sansom, Ian. Paper: an Elegy. New York: Wm. Morrow, 2012.

Seddon, Tony. The Evolution of Type: A Graphic Guide to 100 Landmark Typefaces. Fw. Stephen Coles. Richmond Hill, ON: Firefly, 2015.

Shearer, Karis & Erin Moure. "The Public Reading: Call for a New Paradigm." Public Poetics: Critical Issues in Canadian Poetry and Poetics. Waterloo: Wilfrid Laurier UP, 2015.

Suarez, S.J., Michael F. & H.R. Woudhuysen. The Oxford Companion to The Book, 2 vols. Oxford: Oxford UP, 2010.

Treharne, Elaine, ed. Old and Middle English c. 890-c. 1400: An Anthology, 2nd edn Oxford: Blackwell, 2004.

Weinfield, Henry. The Poet Without a Name: Gray's Elegy and the Problem of History. Carbondale, IL: SIU Press, 1991.

Winchester, Simon. The Professor and the Madman: a Tale of Murder, Insanity, and the Making of The Oxford English Dictionary. New York: HarperPerennial, 1998.

Woods, Tim. The Poetics of the Limit: Ethics & Politics in Modern and Contemporary American Poetry. New York: Palgrave, 2002.

GAZETTEER

The text of GHOST ATLAS is in Andalus
Layout by Gary Anderson using Affinity Publisher
Printed on 70lb premium bond paper

Maps are drawn with ink on Gartner vellum sheets (feuilles de papier vélin / hojas de papel avitelado) 8½ x 11 in (21.6 x 28 cm)

Paintings are acrylic on canvas @ Cover, Mappa Mundi, 16 x 16 in (40.6 x 40.6 cm); Flying Over The Lake In Spring, 9 x 12 in (23 x 30.5 cm); Lost At Sea, 16 x 20 in (40.6 x 50.8 cm); Carta Marina, 14 x 11 in (35.6 x 28 cm); Dispatches/Orisons, 12 x 36 in (30.5 x 91.4 cm); Visitant, 6 x 6 in (15.2 x 15.2 cm) on burlap; The Garden On A Sunny Day, 9 x 12 in (23 x 30.5 cm); both Lost At Sea and The Garden On A Sunny Day are *pentimenti*—canvases initiated by my daughter when she was younger and left unfinished for several years that I have (with her blessing) painted over while retaining the structural features of her original designs (cwtch)

Back cover art by M.A. Slauson, Maya Map, ca. 2010 pen and coloured pencil on paper 6 x 8 in (15.2 x 20.3 cm); author selfies, 2018, 30 Year Old Tie (size 1.77 MB res 1932x2576); Division St., Spokane (size 1.30 MB res 1440x2560)

Photography by Melissa at Voth Photo • www.vothphoto.ca •

CODA

INDEX

Outside there was precisely one folded	53
It took ten technical years for ten years to pass	9
We shot the wind cold full of yellowing syntax	23
You walked onto an adjective not found in the orchid	44
There was a pallor in the sound of its also deep	21
Could I sense a wandering compression in the spine	32
Opined a finch in suburban flutes within seed time	33
Leave everything to the future for now you waited	29
Have everything you need to live by at hand in books	30
Not wanting to be missing it though most important	46
The ease and weight is watching you pacing there	7
Hover back with a breast full of amorous dots	50
See that it happens to you whatever is happening some	37
Childe of the sun in a green glass glowing inside with it	65

The Garden On A Sunny Day

Kurt Slauson is a literary visual artist living in the Okanagan, Kelowna; his first book, INCUNABULAE: COLLECTED WORKS 1990-2015, is also published by Run Amok Books (2017) • www.kurtslauson.com •

www.ingramcontent.com/pod-product-compliance
Lightning Source LLC
Chambersburg PA
CBHW042253100526
44587CB00003B/121